Alfredo

**30
Years, Questions,
Answers.**

Häberli

The Questions 7

No. 1 Thomas Bärnthaler Page 15
What advice do you have for today's young people wishing to become designers?

No. 2 Stephen Bayley Page 19
Can there ever be too much beauty?

No. 3 Tyler Brûlé Page 23
Alfredo, you have long been promising to invite me over for dinner, but as that has yet to happen, I shall invite myself instead. What are we going to eat and drink, and where?

No. 4 Julie Cirelli Page 27
What is the most important public space that should now be preserved?

No. 5 Sarah Douglas Page 32
Your designs embody so much happiness and joie de vivre. What was the happiest moment in your life, and what is your greatest wish for the future?

No. 6 Thomas Edelmann Page 35
Can you remember an idea that was on your mind thirty years ago when you founded your studio? And if so, is it still on your mind now, or has it fallen by the wayside? And if so, why?

No. 7 Meret Ernst Page 40
Alfredo, which of your projects has taught you most about yourself as a designer, and why?

No. 8 Beppe Finessi Page 47
What have you learned from contemporary art for your work as a designer? And what would you advise people interested in design to learn?

The Questions

No. 9 Max Fraser Page 53

The design business has made huge strides over the past thirty years, and the world today is in any case very different. If you were starting up as a designer today, what would you do differently?

No. 10 Chantal Hamaide Page 57

Knowing that you love cars, I'd like to know when you're going to design an electric car or even an entirely new traffic concept? After all, your rich cultural heritage, your understanding of comfort, aesthetics, and technology make you the ideal person to do just that.

No. 11 Hannes Hug Page 63

To paraphrase the famous work by René Magritte:
I see a tree.
What does Alfredo Häberli see?
I see a pipe.
What does Alfredo Häberli see?
I see something that you can't see.
But what do you see?

No. 12 Anniina Koivu Page 65

Which superhero would you like to be? And why?

No. 13 Max Küng Page 67

Which three automobiles would you take with you to a desert island?

No. 14 Soledad Lorenzo Page 74

The painter Pablo Palazuelo said that an artist sees by drawing, and the architect Alberto Campo Baeza says that drawing is "thinking with the hands." Eyes, hands—how would you define it?

30 Years, Questions, Answers. 9

No. 15   Italo Lupi   Page 78

I liked Bruno Munari's works, so how could I not love yours? My question is as follows: To what extent was your work influenced by artists like Bruno and the novelty of freedom with which Italian design unshackled itself from an international style that had degenerated into routine? The idiom of Achille and Piergiacomo Castiglioni must have been music to your ears and undoubtedly a source of inspiration. Is that so?

No. 16   Anna Moldenhauer   Page 84

Alfredo, why is intuitive drawing such a crucial form of expression for you in the creation of your designs?

No. 17   Francesca Molteni   Page 87

These days we talk a lot about inclusion. Why is it still so difficult for women to rise to the top in architecture and design?

No. 18   Hans Ulrich Obrist   Page 91

What are your unrealized projects?

No. 19   Francesca Picchi   Page 95

Given the increasingly homogeneous panoply of goods and products on offer, is there something akin to biodiversity that could be applied to industrial products?

No. 20   Valentina Raggi   Page 98

Your world is a playful and self-conscious cosmos. Multi-disciplinarity, ecology, quantum leaps, and irony are necessary concepts these days, but you have always had them in your DNA. What will be the new symbolic object of tomorrow?

No. 21   Alice Rawsthorn   Page 101

What is design? And what should it be?

The Questions

No. 22 **Sandra Reichl** Page 103

What is passion and what is success?

No. 23 **Erik Rimmer** Page 104

I think of you more than once a week. In fact, I salute you every time I drink wine out of a glass from your Essence collection for Iittala. What was your starting point for that design process? And is there anything you would do differently today?

No. 24 **Marco Sammicheli** Page 108

How would you describe the unknown?

No. 25 **Gunda Siebke** Page 110

What have you done wrong?

No. 26 **David Streiff Corti** Page 113

When did you first realize that you might just make it?

No. 27 **Robert Thiemann** Page 115

How has your focus changed over the past thirty years?

No. 28 **Paolo Tumminelli** Page 118

Imagine your previous life was just a dream and you wake up in a world in which the automobile has not yet been invented. You have to imagine it from scratch. What do you see?

No. 29 **Ramón Úbeda** Page 120

How important is it to have fun when creating—from the first idea to the naming of your work?

No. 30 **Marco Velardi** Page 123

If you had to describe your own personality in terms of food, how would that description read and why?

**30
Years, Questions,
Answers.**

Question No. 1

Thomas Bärnthaler

is an editor at the magazine of the *Süddeutsche Zeitung* and publisher at Phaidon Verlag.

What advice do you have for today's young people wishing to become designers?

The German word for advice, *Ratschlag*, is a portmanteau of two words: *Rat*, meaning counsel, and *Schlag*, meaning a blow or a strike. Consequently, I see a danger of advice striking out in the wrong direction. But what I learned early on, even in the entrance exam and then in the course of my training, is that the profession of designer calls for knowledge and expertise of all kinds. And perhaps talent also plays a part, though how great a part I cannot say. Part of what we do can be learned and this part is larger than we imagine. Designers should be able to notice and to observe things that are not necessarily in plain sight. They must be able to dream and to pursue their dreams doggedly for years at a time. Designers must be courageous enough to put existing knowledge to different uses. And most important of all, they must know themselves well. They must know their own strengths and weaknesses, and be ready to work on changing them where necessary. The task in hand—the content, the outcome—is more important than the designer's own ego. Getting this straight matters not just professionally but in every aspect of life.

The question can also arise indirectly: What is design? What do we regard as design? Is it a finely formed object? An object almost too beautiful to behold? An object that cries out "I was designed?" An object that questions conventions, that tosses traditions overboard? An object that follows a trend?

The history of design began when humans invented tools, weapons, and utensils with which to facilitate a certain activity—hunting, say, or a craft that entailed cutting or carving. They proceeded empirically, treating function and efficiency as paramount. The individual touch—

the decorative, the personal—came later, much, much later. The concept of design arose with industrialization and the forming of artifacts. Today, hundreds of years later, design as a concept has become ubiquitous, which does not make dispensing advice—*Ratschlag*—any easier.

Barricading ourselves inside a study, a lab, a conceptual space might once have been a solution. And there can be no doubt that it resulted in some excellent inventions. The concentration of such a life is almost manic and it still has some justification even today; at times it may even be of the essence. What I've observed over the decades, and can gladly pass on to others, is that these days you have to be incredibly flexible. You have to keep abreast of developments, you have to constantly broaden your skill set, and you have to remain both physically and mentally agile.

For one project, for which I was given just ten minutes in which to prepare a presentation, I developed a kind of manifesto, paring down what I had to say to just a few key points. To become a designer, I said, you needed six Hs: First you need to be Humane, by which I mean ready to do things for others, that is, for society; second, you should be Humble, not arrogant, less me me me and more us us us; this obviously presupposes self–knowledge, and only then can there be Honesty in what you do, and with it transparency vis–à–vis the world; honesty is also a prerequisite for the kind of Holistic approach that is essential to all design work and to the future; then there is the need for Humor, since to see the funny side of things you have to be able to stand apart from them; and, most important of all, you have to have a Heart, by which I mean a passion for doing what you do: searching for an idea, giving it a form, and endowing that form with content.

For me, of course, these six Hs are closely bound up with a seventh: the H of Häberli!

Question No. 2

Stephen Bayley

coined the term "design guru" and founded the successful Boilerhouse project at the V&A Museum in London.

Can there ever be too much beauty?

I became aware of beauty as a concept only when I began working with Italian companies, where the beauty of a product was talked about at some length: *Che bello! Molto bello! Veramente bello! Bellissimo!* My own way of seeing, my own work on ideas, on inventions, on autonomy, was suddenly reduced to a single word: *la bellezza*. And it embraced everything: grace, charisma, attractiveness, style, sophistication, elegance, finesse.

On one occasion we were discussing my Carrara lamp for Luceplan, for example; but Paolo Rizzatto, who in 1978 co-founded Luceplan together with Alessandro Sarfatti, Sandra Severi, and later Alberto Meda, didn't even notice it at first. And that, too, counted as beauty: a corpus as indirect light source standing in an interior and there blending in with its surroundings with grace and elegance. We talked only of beauty. That the molding tool cost a fortune, that it called for what were then the largest parts they had ever molded, that we were using an energy–saving light source for the first time—they were all integral to the lamp's beauty and hence did not warrant any further discussion. For me that was an eye–opener—and a heart–opener.

Why had we not been able to talk about these things while we were in training? I was shaped by my training in Switzerland, a land–locked country, which through its own inventiveness—hidden rationality, a radicalized imagination—was now a player in world trade. Was this rationalization of beauty a result of its having been co–opted by "form follows function"? This revelation was so enlightening to me that other presentations from many years back with Alias, Driade, and Zanotta also began to make sense. Even if those ways of seeing, those discussions, had been about something else. *La bellezza.*

Viewed in this light, we can never have too much beauty.

answers a question by Stephen Bayley

For me it was like learning a new language, the language of beauty. Beauty as a way of seeing. My experience with Japan (perfect imperfection) was very different, and that with Scandinavia (the beauty of light) different again.

But why was it that the buildings in Italy, in Milan, that fascinated me most were those that were strange, different, bizarre, slightly off? Does beauty only become visible when something else is ugly, misshapen, even repellent? That is, by comparison or through contrast? Does ugliness also linger? What ages badly? Can something be unattractive but still possess inner worth? Positive characteristics? An inner beauty? It is for precisely this reason that I sometimes like works of art—sculptures, objects—that are unaesthetic, unappealing, awkward. Because they prompt me to look carefully, and sometimes annoy me, too. Sometimes they are actually an affront to the eyes.

Viewed in this light, we can indeed have too much beauty.

My early travels in Europe in the 1980s, which as a newcomer from Argentina I took advantage of to explore the continent, brought me an abundance of material (magazines, books, exhibitions) which I eagerly lapped up. It was all so extremely inspirational. I had no reservations whatsoever and let everything affect me. And since I didn't really have much of a clue back then, I didn't pass judgment either. All I did was to exercise my powers of perception and to practice interpreting my sensory impressions. This spurred me on to use my own modest means— drawing, in other words—to reflect on those childhood experiences, to lend expression to them, and to process them, as I would do later, more consciously, at the Hochschule für Gestaltung. I never wanted to have a style, a recognizable, visible style. In fact, I hate it with a passion when a form or an aesthetic is applied across the board. So it was sobering for me to see, at my first solo exhibition, how there was in fact a common thread running through all my work as a designer after all. But that feeling of venturing into new terrain that I get with each new blank sheet of paper, each new canvas, is what sustains me in my quest for beauty. Always with the dream of achieving a level of fascination that will touch people.

Question No. 3

Tyler Brûlé

moved from Canada to the UK to launch *Wallpaper* and *Monocle* magazines as a media innovator.

Alfredo, you have long been promising to invite me over for dinner, but as that has yet to happen, I shall invite myself instead.

What are we going to eat and drink, and where?

Did I really promise that? I've never felt the need to publicize my own home. Respect for our private sphere is important to us, to my wife Stefanie, whom you also know, and me. For our friends, of course, we keep open house. You and I have known each other for many years and frequently run into each other in airport lounges, at exhibitions, or at Café Monocle on Dufourstrasse in Zurich, which is in the same part of town as my studio. So we could certainly imagine cooking for you and your partner. I don't know how it is with you guys, but Stefanie and I love being in the kitchen and spend a lot of time there. For me it's more for recreation, and as Monsieur Mise en Place I'm most definitely subordinate to Stefanie as our chef de cuisine.

Cooking is something extremely important to Stefanie's family, too—to her father and even more so her twin brother; likewise to my grandparents with their hotel and my parents with their restaurant. But as a child I was more an onlooker than a doer. The way kitchens work, the clear allocation of roles, the procedures that have to be followed, the movements—it's like being part of a film crew. There has to be a certain symbiosis, as well as clear instructions and clearly defined remits. And what is really important is being able to submit, to take orders. I'm happy to let Stefanie run the show in this domain. The results are just better, it all tastes better—and the kitchen is less likely to fill up with smoke.

So let's start with the drinks, served either in the garden with its views of the lake or in front of the open fire in the living room, and accompanied by strips of toasted bread with various homemade toppings: tartar, fish, and asparagus or artichoke mousse. All the ingredients come from the market at Bürkliplatz.

Next we'll have starters of the season. For that I would suggest lots of little oval plates of beetroot carpaccio with horseradish foam, beef carpaccio with Parmesan shavings, seafood salad, salmon carpaccio with yuzo sauce, cooked and peeled peperoni rolled up and filled with cream cheese, olives with lemon zest, bufala with rucola, preserved shallots, and so forth.

Then just a very small portion of homemade ravioli, or a lemongrass soup with coriander. And as a main course, slow-cooked veal with jus de morille and fresh vegetables.

Dessert could be served in front of the fire again, or, depending on how we feel, at the large oval Wegner table made of wood. As wine I'd suggest a Franciacorta from the Brescia region (Alias' home turf) and an Ojo de Agua cuvée grown by my neighbor Dieter Meier.

The coffee will be from Schwarzenbach, the colonial goods store in the Old Town.

The table will be decorated with fresh flowers in little bottles, several Tris candelabras, a fine linen tablecloth and serviettes, and, best of all, tableware from my *Fluen* series for Fürstenberg.

For dessert there will be cheesecake, which Stefanie does really well, and a dulce de leche cake made according to one of my mother's recipes.

The guests might also include Vera and Lars, whom you know from their column in *Konfekt Magazine,* but were perhaps not aware are neighbors of ours? And perhaps Konstantin and Katharina with Carla and Kasimir will also be able to join us. Or it will just be the six of us—not to forget our cats Pitschi and Uno.

Question No. 4

Julie Cirelli

is co–director of Park Books in Switzerland and has written various books on design.

What is the most important public space that should now be preserved?

The question is an extremely controversial one given all that has been written and predicted about the foreseeable future. With our cities becoming ever more populous and the countryside draining of people, living space is becoming horrendously expensive, forcing us to make do with less of it than we would like; hence the ever greater importance of the public space as a space for everyone.

The street as a public space was one of the subjects I discussed in my future mobility project *The Sphere—Perspectives in Precision & Poetry* for

BMW, 2015. *The Sphere* is a graphic vision of the paths that will connect us in the future. But these will no longer be the lanes, roads, and highways made of dirt, paving stones, and asphalt that are familiar to us today. Nor will they lead simply from A to B, because they will not be linear. They will not even be real. *The Sphere* is conceived more like a three-dimensional Facebook; a kind of endless loop that is constantly in motion; an abstract, seemingly boundless and flat skate park landscape on which real-life social contacts can be formed and cultivated. What will the route described by a text message—from Europe to Asia, say—actually look like? And which route will an image sent to Africa take?

What interests me is the visual image that emerges from all this, which is rather like the trajectory of an airplane or a bird, but three-dimensional. At times, the concept underlying it seems to me to be vague; but at other times it is very real, becoming sharp, vivid, and clear again. Might these paths be organic, circuitous? Is it conceivable that cities will one day rise up out of a large, horizontal expanse, like mountains out of a sea of fog—a sight we all know well? What soars up into the sky might be a mountain, or a giant forest, or an island paradise, or a city.

And what if all the movement, all the activity, were on a lower level with the residential space above it? What kind of an image would that produce? *The Sphere* sought a different kind of image for the surface on which the ship is gliding along—a surface that is not made of clouds, nor of seawater, nor even of air. Nor is it made of plastic, like Federico Fellini's magnificent rendition of the sea in *E la nave va* (And the Ship Sails On).

Green spaces, parks, and recreational areas are all vitally important to the city. And it is not just air quality that they improve, but also the mental health of city–dwellers. As unavoidable as the massive densification of cities may yet become, it seems to me that we will still need paths, streets, and even *The Sphere* itself running through them. By this I mean streets, cycle paths, sidewalks, and metro lines, although the means by which we get from A, as the place where we sleep, to B, as the place where we work, is just as important. Together they form a public space that is used in many different ways, with many different media, and many different vehicles. This space seems to me to pose a greater challenge than would a park or a green space. It is actually more a political concern. But how will our means of transport develop in the future? And how important will they be to us?

As for *The Sphere* street, there are social components to it that warrant closer attention on grounds of their potential to facilitate encounters with other people and the co-existence of completely different speeds that they permit. Whenever we spend time outdoors, weather and pandemic restrictions permitting, we soon become aware of how the spaces between buildings are brought to life by movement—walking, running, cycling—and by the social encounters that take place on benches, in cafés, and such like. The repurposing of a metro line, the remodeling of a six-lane highway, a rerouted and disused highway through a city—these are all opportunities to create a different kind of public space.

Here there are no limits to what the human imagination might come up with. My only reservations have to do with how these spaces are used. We must respect them, because they belong to us all, and matter to us all, too. An unbuilt lot, an open space, a public square can be conceived either as a more or less private space or—depending on how accessible it is, who uses it, who controls it, who maintains it, and what their responsibilities are—as a public space (from Territorial Claims, by Herman Hertzberger). Translating public and private in terms of who bears responsibility makes things easier, in other words. The key to connecting domains with divergent territorial claims, and hence our passage from one to the other, is the threshold, that interstitial space that as a place in its own right is also a prerequisite for encounters and dialogue between the two.

So the aim should be to create such in–between spaces, even if people on the street feel that they are no concern of theirs, and even if such a system gives rise to a widespread sense of alienation.

Sarah Douglas

Question No. 5

is editor–in–chief of *Wallpaper* magazine and a connector in the global design community.

Your designs embody so much happiness and joie de vivre. What was the happiest moment in your life, and what is your greatest wish for the future?

As a teenager perusing an art magazine I chanced on a quote from Roy Lichtenstein, an artist famous for his blown–up comic–book scenes, which was to have a formative influence on me. It went something like this: "You have to have the courage to go after happiness. Courage doesn't come out of thin air, but if you don't seize it, you'll regret it later on."

I think this struck a chord in me because as a teenager on the cusp of adulthood I was still searching for myself, and perhaps also because that was the first time I realized just what a happy childhood I had had in Argentina and how much I owed my parents and their families. I have believed in my gift for embracing happiness ever since, and this is reflected, I hope, in both who I am and what I do, even allowing for all the hard work, persistence, and professionalism behind it. My own manifesto, which also underscores the need for courage in order to be happy, goes like this: "Say what you do. Do what you say. And be what you do."

Over the thirty years in which design has shaped my life, I have had the indescribable pleasure of meeting people who have guided me and even changed the course of my life. I am currently writing this book about some of these encounters. It's about the people themselves. This relatively calm phase in which the world now is for me is an opportunity to view things differently and to question things that I've hitherto taken for granted. And I do not believe that we can simply return to business as usual. The big question is rather: What is truly indispensable? Right now I'm reviewing the past and writing about my own experiences.

One indescribable happiness was the birth of our children. Those are moments when nature, fate, and happiness all come together in a harmonious whole. A moment of happiness beyond comprehension! And the one I have to thank for that is my wife, who bore us two wonderful children. That instant of becoming a father, of taking responsibility as a father, gave my life a purpose and a meaning. More than I would ever have dreamed possible. And it also put my work as a designer into perspective, which is perhaps why my most fruitful period came after that.

My greatest wish for the future of my children, and all young people, is that they find something that they enjoy and that it brings them happiness and fulfilment. Of course our lives are to a large degree shaped by circumstances. But I'm still a firm believer in happiness—for which you nevertheless need courage.

Question No. 6

Thomas Edelmann

directed *Design Report* magazine and is now a freelance journalist, critic, and curator in Hamburg.

Can you remember an idea that was on your mind thirty years ago when you founded your studio? And if so, is it still on your mind now, or has it fallen by the wayside? And if so, why?

When I first took the entrance exam for the Hochschule für Gestaltung, I was one of over two hundred applicants and several dozen exam candidates. When I was not among the top twelve and had to content myself with the number thirteen spot, the anguish was unbearable; though it also hardened my resolve to try again a year later, when I was accepted. My German was just as bad as before, but I was rewarded for having given it another shot. Among those who prompted my choice of profession was Achille Castiglioni, an architect from Milan, whose products fascinated me—or rather drove me crazy!

When my graduation project won me the very lucrative Hochschule Prize 1991 (my revenge for my lousy German!), I was so elated that I grabbed the telephone and called Castiglioni to thank him. The very next day he invited me over for coffee at his studio at Piazza Castello 27. Luckily for me there were enough trains from Zurich to Milan to get me there on time. Instead of the ten minutes originally agreed, my visit actually lasted all afternoon. Castiglioni emptied the display cases containing his collection of objects and told me all sorts of stories about them. He gesticulated so fast that all the black–and–white photos I took of him with my Minox 35 GT are out of focus. Several years later I had a similar experience with Bruno Munari. Never before had I encountered such vitality at such a great age. Both men were models beyond compare!

I asked Castiglioni if I could work for him, which after all was my dream. Realizing that I had taken the train from Zurich specially to ask him this one question, he expressed surprise. He actually had no wish to enlarge his small team, he said, and even if he had, he would doubtless choose a personal friend like the Swiss graphic artist Max Huber, or Italo Lupi, or the architect Michele de Lucchi, all of whom I fortunately got to know later on. Castiglioni's advice to me personally, however, was to open a studio of my own. Because the only other Swiss designer he knew was Mario Botta, who was really an architect. Castiglioni also assured me that being a designer was the most wonderful profession in the world.

I opened my studio at Hardturmstrasse 68 in Zurich the very next day.

Obviously I had had plenty of time to think it over on the train back from Milan. But I also had no Plan B. There was only Plan A, which was to set up my own studio. And that Castiglioni himself had suggested it made me even more determined. It was what I felt and what I thought and what I did all rolled into one. And it was a good fit, too, since being employed would have clipped my wings, restricted my conceptual world, and my vision. Only Milan was a place of inspiration. There was no design office in Zurich that held any fascination for me. And the time was ripe: 1991.

Today, three decades later, I would do it all over again. And I would urge young people to go their own way, too. Whether that means being self–employed I cannot say, since running a design studio has become infinitely more complex in the meantime. By going their own way, I mean that young people should get to know themselves, find out what they do well, what they're passionate about, and then go for it. That's what I spent my apprenticeship as an architectural draftsman, my time at college, and my internship doing, because it takes time.

Perhaps these days the possibilities are so many and varied that a whole range of options can be considered, making for a lack of direction. I've always said that had I not become a designer I would have become a cartoonist or an engineer:

always using a minimum of means to maximum effect, wordlessly, or working with materials. These days I would learn a trade, perhaps become a stonemason, a sculptor, a writer—best of all a philosopher! But for that I would need an extra–long train journey to no–man's–land!

Meret Ernst

Question No. 7

was editor of *Hochparterre* magazine and is currently a lecturer in design at HGK Basel.

Alfredo, which of your projects has taught you most about yourself as a designer, and why?

Probably that would be the projects that were never actually realized, often because just one little thing, one tiny piece of a hugely complex design process, didn't work. Those are the projects that brought me down.

But I also learned a lot—including about myself—during my internships for Nick Roericht in Ulm (1988) and at Siemens in New York (1988-1989), both of which I chose specifically to find out what I was really interested in—whether it was capital goods in medicine or telecommunications or more the kind of conceptual work and studies done by Roericht. Then while at college I deliberately chose to do a shoe project with Bally and then my graduation project with felt, which was all about tranquility.

I wanted to bring felt back out into the open, to have it play the lead role as a load–bearing material. I wanted to use it as a valuable, high–end material. The overarching theme was tranquility, and I decided to take felt as my starting point after discovering Joseph Beuys's 1965 sculpture *Schneefall* at Kunstmuseum Basel. My professors warned me that I ran the risk of ending up empty–handed, and I was aware of that, too. But I believed in what I was doing and was willing to stake everything on that one material. Amazingly, there was no pressure at all and I was able to go with the flow. In the end, I presented a recliner, a lounge chair, a rug, a parabruit (a screen to keep out noise), and a poncho, all of which won me the lucrative Hochschule Prize for the best graduation project of my year.

I spent those last three years at college and the internship following my instincts, my dreams, my vision—consistently, relentlessly, even, but without ever forfeiting my enjoyment. I had built up such a head of steam over the years, especially after failing the entrance exam first time round, that I was like a boomerang bouncing back. Since my great weakness was German, I had to let my works speak for me. That was in any case my thing: objects that people commune with, domestic objects, interiors, capsules, houses, clothes.

Several years later I learned what royalties contracts are; and how collaboration with Italian firms works; and what it means to follow a dream year after year, fair after fair, visit after visit. No school, no design program can teach you that. The young designer opening a studio on day one after graduation is faced with the school of life.

My approach was actually the same as I would later apply to various projects and exhibitions. Obviously, I was greatly helped by what I'd learned from my many joint exhibitions with Martin Heller, especially the question: "What are you working on? What is it all about?" This recurring question, which homes in on the essence of what designers do, has helped me with every one of my projects, no matter how insecure I might have felt vis–à–vis the design industry, as someone working in a different country, in a different language. Over and over again, that question enabled me to reactivate that image, that feeling of having nothing to lose. It was just as it had been in Argentina: I took things a day at a time, then a week, a month, a year, always taking each day as it came, but with humor, with joy. This approach to life, necessitated by Argentina's dire political and economic situation, has helped me enormously.

But the first projects also entailed a fair amount of pain and anguish. Sometimes it had to do with the quality of the end product. Sometimes it was my being unable to correct the prototypes yet again. And sometimes it was the feeling of not being properly understood. By then I was no longer working solo as I had done at college, because developing prototypes naturally entails working with engineers, technicians, industry, corporations, clients. But I learned something new every time. I analyzed the disappointments and drew my own conclusions from them. My goal was always to do better next time, and for sure not to make the same mistakes again. And that's still how it is today, since the range we cover in the studio is huge. We're constantly venturing into new terrain. So the courage to work on something new has never left me. On the contrary, the less familiar a project is, the more exciting I find it.

Every new project begins with me sitting in front of a blank sheet of paper, facing the void. One reason I became a designer was that design is a field in which personal emotions and experience have a direct bearing on your work. Designs are conceived by humans for humans.

The program at the Hochschule für Gestaltung was conceived to be very broad in scope. I came to it as a trained architectural draftsman who had learned design at vocational school and done some painting early on—so with wide-ranging interests that I still have today. My aim was never to become a jack of all trades, which is how Swiss designers are sometimes disparagingly described, although that says more about the speakers' envy than about them.

I had to get to know myself, my pleasures and passions, my powers of endurance, and my limitations. I understood right from the start that what my training was ultimately all about was enabling me to know myself better. Design and interiors were my priorities, of course, but the most important thing, in my view, was getting to know myself.

Which themes were of interest to me?
What did I want to work on?
What did I want to change?
And who for?
What was my standpoint?
What was my take?
How would I set myself apart?
What were my strengths?
My weaknesses?

A comparison with a tennis player might prove revealing here, since sport is also about constantly learning to do things better and to try out new things. Of course there will always be that one match, or in my case that one project, that turns out to be a watershed, a steep learning curve. Such projects certainly exist. I learned an incredible amount from my first products for an Italian client that actually went into production—that was for D. House / Driade in 1995. Then there was the first time I used plastic, meaning that tools had to be made, my first glasses, rubber parts, die–cast aluminum. And once my designs started going into production and being marketed worldwide, I had to learn to take responsibility, indirectly, both for the design itself and for the end product. That first time I had to take responsibility as a designer I didn't sleep a wink from Friday to

Monday, but spent the whole weekend at the studio, checking every detail in time for delivery on Monday. There was a lot of money at stake, as the client had had to invest heavily in tools.

But it was that same project that made me grow up. Perhaps at the time it was too much and far exceeded my abilities as a young designer, but opportunities like that are unique; and the experience did not deter me from taking on even larger projects: an entire hotel, 130 rooms, six floors, sixty new products; or the design of an electric car, both inside and out, complete with dashboard and a new motor concept. Then there was the study of an ensemble of houses to meet the most exacting environmental and energy–saving standards in Europe. They were all great learning experiences. And I could never have mastered any of them had I not known myself. Because finding order in this universe, in this emotional chaos, that is the challenge facing the designer—the challenge of life itself.

Question No. 8

Beppe Finessi

is an architect, PhD holder, and active in teaching, criticism, and research in Italy.

What have you learned from contemporary art for your work as a designer? And what would you advise people interested in design to learn?

I was deeply honored when the 2006 Biennale Interieur in Kortijk selected me to be its guest of honor. I was the first Swiss designer to be accorded this distinction, apart from Vitra CEO Rolf Fehlbaum in 1998—and Rolf isn't even a designer!

So I decided to use the 5,000 square meters placed at my disposal not just to exhibit my own work, but also to showcase Swiss design generally. I was determined to show something different. So not only did I exhibit 280 objects from the design collection of the Museum für Gestaltung Zürich, but together with seven Swiss artists and the publisher Birkhäuser Verlag I produced the book *Alfredo Häberli Design Live,* the subject of which was not my work as a designer, but rather what those seven artists saw in it. I presented my own products in a large architectural installation and chose the artists in consultation with my friend the art director Beda Achermann. Our aim was to generate variety and to make the content as exciting as possible. They included sculptors, painters, and photographers, and they all took one of my products as a starting point for a work of their own. Our choreography amounted to nothing more than giving the artists the products, which varied considerably in both size and type.

The artists were Shirana Shahbazi, David Renggli, Walter Pfeiffer, Roman Signer, John M Armleder, Körner Union, and Stefan Burger. Since I knew them all from their work, and personally, too, I was able to visit them in their studios or have them visit me in mine. So there was an ongoing dialogue both with the artists and with Achermann. We got to know each other well and in some cases became firm friends. The most exciting and most revealing part of the project was comparing what I had imagined with the actual results. Which of my products will they want? What will the one or the other of them be interested in? What will they make of it? How will their works turn out? What kind of personalities am I dealing with? In the end there was everything from maximum precision to sloppiness, friendliness to arrogance, professionalism to naivete. Seeing what today's creative pantheon was capable of was very revealing.

The work supplied by Roman Signer was remarkable for its exceptional modesty, humanity, and humor, which is what struck me about him when I visited him. We brought several more tables, which we had in the studio. So when unloading, he kindly but firmly pointed out that he had "ordered only one" and that the rest of it didn't have to be unloaded at all. Admittedly, at our next visit, he wanted to order a sofa, too, and a series of glasses. And I gave him a different table that he was very glad of and able to make use of. He's so incredibly modest in manner, so witty in the way he talks, so acute in the way he thinks, and so innovative in what he does. I developed tremendous esteem for him, and he reminded me very much of Bruno Munari, including those fine sketches of his.

In 2008 I visited Roman with Anders Byriel, CEO of the Danish firm Kvadrat, who is a connoisseur of Roman's oeuvre and a great fan of his. Byriel wanted to gift a work by Roman to the Louisiana Museum just outside Copenhagen—which incidentally is one of the most beautiful museums in Europe. If possible, he wanted it to be something with textiles worked into it since Kvadrat makes textiles for high-end designers. Roman doesn't do any advertising, which was not Byriel's idea in any case. But the following summer they made a video of five rockets catapulting a 50-meter-long bolt of cloth over the beach and into the sea at Ebeltoft, where Kvadrat is headquartered. So that was the beginning of their collaboration and friendship. Mine was already established.

As a designer I've learned—or rather have had it confirmed to me—that the way artists work is no different than the way architects, fashion designers, and designers generally work: It's all about ideas, about putting ideas into practice, and being a human. The only difference is the context, which is freer for artists, even if their actual content, as opposed to its realization, is subject to similar restrictions. What I most definitely learned from Roman (who incidentally has the same background as me in that he also trained as an architectural draftsman) was this: He chose a non-commercial medium, by which I mean videos of his own performances, and has stuck to it without wavering. That so many young artists today regard him as a role model is therefore unsurprising. He is a role model for me, too, and a source of strength, especially in the field of design, which is very much controlled by marketing.

I learned a lot from the other artists, too: from Shirana Shahbazi about precision in photography, which she does incredibly well; from David Renggli about wit, surprise, and a visual lightness of touch; from Walter Pfeiffer about sensitivity, high-quality aesthetics, and color; from Stefan Burger about intellectuality (somewhere between Goethe and Kippenberger) and empathy; from John M Armleder about aesthetic perfection; and from Körner Union about the youthful observation of an object.

I have also had the great good fortune, indeed the honor, to make the acquaintance of very different personalities from architecture and design who have been just as fascinating. I'm thinking here of Enzo Mari, Bruno Munari, Achille Castiglioni, and Italo Lupi, from whom I've learned all sorts of things, and all of whom planted seeds in me.

Question No. 9

Max Fraser

is a London–based curator and consultant who writes design books for publishers around the world and joined *Dezeen* as editorial director in 2023.

The design business has made huge strides over the past thirty years, and the world today is in any case very different. If you were starting up as a designer today, what would you do differently?

Would I not be as radical, as unyielding, as vision–driven as I was back then? Would I make more compromises, be more mainstream, and for that better off? Of course, I now have so much more experience to draw on that I probably would do things differently. But how?

First we must acknowledge that industry has changed, in that many of those small businesses that perhaps used to be suppliers at some point noticed that since they knew the designers, too, they could do much of the work themselves. In the early days of my studio there were ten major producers, most of them family businesses run by just one person, a *grande imprenditore* who had the talent, intuition, courage, audacity, and stamina to work in dialogue with architects and later with designers on the development of highly sophisticated, idealistic, visionary products. Sales were not a worry, at least not initially, because back then you let the magazines, the books, the newspapers, and the trade fairs do the marketing for you.

Those ten major producers have since been joined by hundreds of others. And electronic communications and smart gadgetry have made the marketing more important than the actual products, with designers and architects hyped as stars. Many family businesses run by a single "genius" did not survive the transition to the next generation and were snapped up by the investment groups that now dominate the furnishings and interior design business. So it seems as if that chapter is ending—and a new one beginning.

Design should reclaim its true mission, its mission as a cultural statement, and be willing to engage in critique. But as in the automotive industry, fashion, art, and architecture, the principal content of our society is now business—which is dispiriting, but true.

But back to the question: What would I do differently? Perhaps fight harder for an ideal that is worth fighting for? I had been friends with Enzo Mari for many years when I realized I had to distance myself from him. His outrageous, trenchant, and vital critique and his fighting spirit were unique in the design community. But for me as a much younger designer, they were almost paralyzing. I wanted to take up the fight, but in a positive way and without forfeiting my enjoyment.

As a young designer today, I would be more interested in the environment, in ecology, biology, and people. I would also take a deep dive into the concept of degrowth. That said, these things only make sense when tackled in partnership with industry and business. And for that the outlook is good.

Thirty years ago I was able to fulfill my dream of first studying and then working in design.

These days you have to be flexible, to be constantly learning new skills, and exploring professions that didn't even exist back then. Training in design is a great basis for that. So I think I'd do it all over again even today. The path taken would be a different one, though exactly how, or what, I cannot say. The philosopher Søren Kierkegaard said: "Life can only be understood by looking backward, but it must be lived looking forward."

Question No. 10

Chantal Hamaide

founded the internationally reporting design magazine *Intramuros* in Paris.

Knowing that you love cars, I'd like to know when you're going to design an electric car or even an entirely new traffic concept? After all, your rich cultural heritage, your understanding of comfort, aesthetics, and technology make you the ideal person to do just that.

My engagement with the mobility of the future began when BMW commissioned me to design a project of my own invention. That resulted in my creation of *The Sphere,* a kind of three-dimensional composite, and *The Vessel,* which was not a car, not a plane, not a boat—but more a dynamic house. Then there was *The Dwell,* the protective home and place of refuge, and finally *The Couch,* which seems to be the soul of the house.

As for the inside of the *The Vessel: These Perspectives in Precision & Poetry* about the mobility of the future and its influence on cities, streets, how we live, and how we get from A to B, this inquiry in the form of large and small models, drawings and sketches, wall reliefs, area models, illustrations, and a skeleton vehicle built to scale plus the accompanying pamphlet so impressed the BMW board and BMW designers that I was awarded a follow-up contract, entrusting me, their only external designer, with the creation, from start to finish, of a new electric SUV. I had at my disposal a team of a dozen or so engineers, transport designers, computer graphics experts, and model-builders, and together we developed an exterior model, an interior model, and a cockpit with a fully functional interface. The content was manifesto-like, as was the stance of our "Team H." The H stood for Humble, Human, and Honest, but also for Humor and Heart—not to mention Häberli and Hampf, with whom I shared the leadership of the team.

The SUV had two rows of seats for three people each, and the rear seat could be moved all the way to the back to create a kind of stretch–limo effect, or a long version with plenty of legroom. The floor of the vehicle was completely flat, and together with the engineers we developed a new electric drive. Especially important to me was that the Monovan be friendly, modest, and scaled down in size. We developed it from the inside out and arrived at an astonishingly spacious end result. So my work as the external designer was done.

It took the automotive industry, especially the Germans, far too long to take electrification seriously. Their attitude was one of arrogant disdain and designers from outside the industry were treated with condescension. But I have gasoline in my blood! After all, I grew up just three kilometers away from a racetrack and cars had a formative influence on me as a boy. But I'm veering off the topic and haven't actually answered your question.

I'm generally a great fan of sailboats, as the wind that powers them is wholly natural. I'm fascinated by gliders for the same reason, especially those that experiment with solar power, and bicycles, too, which are driven by muscle power. That's why my Vessel turned out to be a cross between a hull, an aircraft with rigid sails, and a car.

For as much as the current bicycle boom is a good thing, I still find e-bikes disappointing. They're designed for a quick sell, welded and cobbled together out of off-the-shelf components. Horrible! Of course there are one or two really excellent models, but the vast bulk of them are a missed opportunity.

And given the sheer quantity of trendy rental scooters, cars, motorbikes, buses, and trams currently cluttering up our cities, our public spaces are beginning to look like disaster zones. Many things are developing too fast for sensible solutions to be developed, including computers and electrification. This is an exciting challenge and a huge field in which there is a lot of work to be done, especially for young designers.

I don't have a solution to it, although I have observed the following: The younger generations would like to own less, and many of them see no point in learning to drive. Even those who do often use their license just to rent a car now and then and actually own two bicycles instead. What is clear is that there are alternative ways of getting around, at least in the city, even if individual locomotion is here to stay and sharing remains difficult. When objects do not belong to us personally, we soon stop taking care of them, as can be seen in the treatment of e–scooters, subways, park benches, and bus stops.

So we'll have to find solutions on several different levels. There are certainly enough questions: What will happen to our streets, to our boulevards, once cars have been banished from our cities? And how far out of the city does a metro have to go? Will we then have car silos, or, better still, bike silos? And if I travel from the station to the office using a two– or four–wheeled electric vehicle, where will I park it? Will it make any difference if I only commute into town on three days a week and otherwise work from home? Should this be a matter for my employer? Or the state? Would drones be an answer to the problem of congestion?

We've developed hybrids between a balance bike and scooter for very young children, as well as soapbox cars and whole catalogues of safety concepts for the automotive industry. We've also fine-tuned city bikes to make them more nimble, and have developed real cars like the ones I spoke of earlier. One project that's currently under discussion is for a short– to medium–range compact electric car.

So while I can't provide a concrete answer to the question, I know for sure that there will be solutions. We just don't have them in our heads yet.

Question No. 11

Hannes Hug

is a Zurich resident by choice, a media worker for Swiss radio and television, and lives free– and left–handed.

To paraphrase the famous work by René Magritte: I see a tree. What does Alfredo Häberli see? I see a pipe. What does Alfredo Häberli see? I see something that you can't see. But what do you see?

I see a hammock held aloft by balloons with me lying in it, arms casually akimbo behind my head, gazing up at the clouds that make for such a contrast with the bright blue sky of Argentina. A bird has alighted on one of the wooden bars and lets the balloons lift it up into the unending expanse of the sky and clouds, and later the stars. That's what I see. And this image takes me away with it, becoming smaller and smaller, and eventually disappearing into thin air.

And as a designer I would like to make that thin air visible.

Question No. 12

Anniina Koivu

is a design writer, curator, consultant, and lecturer who commutes between Milan and Lausanne.

Which superhero would you like to be? And why?

My superhero could well be Pippi Longstocking, even if I got to know her—the book, the films, and the stories, that is—only as an adult together with my own children. To give her her full name: Pippilotta Victualia Rollgardina Peppermint Ephraimsdotter Longstocking.

I like her self–confidence and her impudence; the character traits that she possesses are traits that I myself would like to retain in my old age. I also like her charisma, and as a designer the fact that she is a searcher after things. Thinking of my studio as a kind of cabinet of curiosities, I'm sure that

Pippilotta Victualia Rollgardina Peppermint Ephraimsdotter Longstocking would like it here. Her monkey friend Mr. Nilsson could climb on the shelves and we'd have room even for her horse.

Question No. 13

Max Küng

grew up on a farm in Switzerland, is an author, and writes texts and columns for *Das Magazin*.

Which three automobiles would you take with you to a desert island?

It's frowned upon these days, but I have to confess that I'm a real automobile aficionado. I grew up just three kilometers away from a racetrack and my brother and I were in and out of the pits all the time. After all, we were the sons of Don Alfredo, and my parents' restaurant was where the drivers and team owners generally ate. I could identify every car just by the noise of its engine. My uncle and father also took us to watch road races and my uncle drew pictures of the cars he spotted in European magazines. Argentina was always crazy about car–racing. My Matchbox cars were the only toys I took with me to Switzerland, even though I no longer played with them, and I still have that shoebox full of them. It was because of the Iso Grifo No. 14 in the Lesley Matchbox series that I became a designer, at least indirectly. That's because the cars I would like best later on in Europe were all designed by Giorgetto Giugiaro: the Alfa Romeo Alfetta GTV, the first VW Golf, the Fiat Panda, and the Fiat Uno. Many years later, I was a juror alongside Walter Da Silva, Stephen Bayley, and Giorgetto Giugiaro at a concours d'elegance, the first Schloss Bensberg Classics of 2009. What an honor that was!

And what an honor, and a delight, when Giugiaro himself, on hearing about my background and what I was doing at the time, showed me his concept for the 1973 Audi Asso di Picche. He knew it all by heart, and it was all still fully functional, even the engine. That design, now all but forgotten, was remarkable for its sharp nose and very flat hood and windshield. The body angled in so sharply that they had to develop a special mechanism for winding down the windows. The cockpit was similar to Mario Bellini's 1972 Divisumma 18 Electronic for Olivetti and the interior was lavishly upholstered in "crinkly" leather. Then there were those door pockets attached with snap fasteners that could be taken out and used as handbags—

classic seventies design. Giugiaro was thirty-four when he conceived the design, and his mischievous smile at the time was of a piece with his creation. Our discussion in 2009 was one of the highlights of my life as a designer.

Working on various projects for the automotive industry over the years enabled me to immerse myself ever deeper in the history of car design. Architecture, art, fashion, and furniture design I knew well, which is why my discovery of concept cars took my breath away. I found whole books on the subject (such as *500 voitures extraordinaires* or *Voiture de rêve*) and in them all sorts of designs by people I'd never heard of. Nor did my attempts to find out more about them yield much of substance.

So if the only three shoes you need are a loafer, a Chelsea, and an Oxford, and the three watches one for everyday wear, an elegant timepiece for going out, and something sporty for sports and leisure, your fleet of cars should perhaps comprise one Italian, one English, and one German model—especially if designed by Giugiaro, Marcello Gandini, or Pininfarina. There's something exciting about such triads and triangles—like the Bermuda Triangle in which everything we think and know disappears.

Our first car was a light–blue Fiat 128, which my then girlfriend and now wife Stefanie and I inherited from her great–aunt. Years later we were so panicked about our financial situation that we ended up selling it. So off it went to the azure skies of Greece, which is where the buyer lived. Later, after our son was born, we bought a Golf GTD. Then I bought myself a Saab Turbo Cabriolet, which I still have today, and a Saab 9–5 TQT as a family car. For my fiftieth birthday Stefanie gave me a Ferrari 456 GT, which after a good deal of agonizing I traded in for a 1977 Porsche 911.

But back to the question. Perhaps it would be interesting to insert an additional level of motorization? Four, six, eight, or even twelve cylinders? Electric? And what about those Argentinian cars like IKA Renault's Torino? You really are asking the impossible. Only three?! I'd dearly like to know how you'd handle it, although it's probably much easier for a *Tages–Anzeiger* columnist and author of books. So how would it be if you were limited to just three bikes? Ah, now it's getting difficult for you, too!

To return to my collection of Matchbox cars: The most angular of them after the Iso Grifo was the Alfa Romeo Carabo with its purple body and yellow chassis, and the Lamborghini Marzal with its pink body and yellow windows.

I later saw all these cars for real, on a scale of one to one: the Carabo at the Alfa Romeo Museum in Varese and the Marzal, of which there is only one in existence, on Lake Como in 2019. It's comforting to know that it now belongs to a Swiss collection.

But even the proportions of the Mini with its centered exhaust pipe were of interest to me. And there were some American models that also stood out, like the Ford Mustang, Ford 100 Pick Up, and the Mercury station wagon with the dogs peering out the back. So that was my world of automobiles.

When the magazine *Architektur & Wohnen* named me Designer of the Year, I had some of my Matchbox cars photographed and then plotted them on a scale of one to one, pairing each toy car with its "real" counterpart— which is how the scratches, the fat tires, the oversized A–pillars, and the colors came to be such powerfully emotive factors in the show *Der Design–Playboy:* The Designer who Plays.

If I had to select three models of the same brand, it would be a 911 Targa, a Macan, and a Taycan. So everyday use, sportiness, and elegance that all go by the same name: Porsche.

But that was not the thrust of the question, which was rather about the three cars that I would choose for life, that I would take with me on Noah's Ark? When the question is put this way, I find myself playing the contrarian. If everyone else says A, then I start searching for a B. We all know the kind of furniture, the kind of watches whose selection and purchase require no courage at all, that have been chosen for us—by history, by good taste, by popular appeal. Statistics.

Just think of how wonderfully friendly the R4 and R5 were, the elegance and comfort of a Citroën SM or CX Pallas, a Rover 3500. Autonomy is something that has always interested me—autonomy as in the AMC Pacer or Gremlin, or the Saab 900, which you either love or hate, never anything in between. That is why of all the Lamborghinis, the one I liked best was the Jarama, in part because so little is ever said about it. Then there's the Fiat 8V Zagato or Maserati A6G/2000 Berlinetta Zagato (1956), the Abarth 205, and Ferrari 250 SWB, or Marcello Gandini's Bravo P114, and his truly astounding Miura, Countach, and Stratos. I'm also a big fan of shooting brakes, which is why I quite like the contemporary Ferrari FF Lusso, even if the design has not been well received.

So it remains a *question de rêve,* or perhaps a *question de cauchemar.*

Perhaps in the end my choice
would be as follows:

a 1962 Ferrari 250 GT SWB
Berlinetta Speciale (designed by Giorgetto Giugiaro),

a 1974 Fiat 130 Maremma
shooting brake (by Pininfarina), and

a 1974 Aston Martin Lagonda
in William Towns's "folded paper" style

—or wait, maybe

a 1979 Aston Martin Bulldog
after all?

Soledad Lorenzo

Question No. 14

is a Spanish art historian who publishes books and magazines on design and architecture.

The painter Pablo Palazuelo said that an artist sees by drawing, and the architect Alberto Campo Baeza says that drawing is "thinking with the hands."

Eyes, hands— how would you define it?

Alfredo Häberli

I like the idea of taking a line for a walk.

My Swiss grandfather George Häberli always did quiet things with us, so whenever we were at his place we did things like fishing, learning to swim, jumping off a diving board, and drawing. The first step was to relax the hand, which we did by filling a whole sheet with endless rings of more or less equal size, going in one direction on one sheet and in the opposite direction on the next. Then came the loops and swoops and figures like musical notation, which all had to be done by a single sweep of the hand, both clockwise and counterclockwise. It was all completely calm—silent, in fact. These warmup exercises served not only to calm us down and to loosen up the wrist, but also, most important of all, to empty the head. We were to think of nothing but the line, the pencil, the blank sheet of paper, or of nothing at all. It was drawing from the guts. That's why I say that every child draws intuitively, directly, wonderfully.

After that, we went outdoors and drew whatever we saw there. Those weekends were a dream. I believe that was the first time I took a line for a walk; it just came along of its own accord! Many years later I was in the life drawing class at the Hochschule für Gestaltung, where as one of our exercises we were given just ten seconds to capture a nude figure on paper; long enough for about three strokes—but what expressive strokes they were! And there it was: a new position; and then another ten seconds for another one. I kept some of those drawings and still have them now. And I often think back to those times with my grandfather.

When I take a line for a walk today, then it is on several different levels, since I use the medium of drawing on three different levels: First I draw for myself. These drawings can be poetic without any particular purpose at all, because a sketchbook is a kind of visual diary. On the second level, drawing—or rather sketching—is my way of teasing out ideas for a new product. Third, I need sketches or drawings to help me when words are no longer adequate, such as when I'm trying to explain what I want to engineers. One of sketching's most important functions is to make our own ideas comprehensible. And drawing is essential when explaining things. Besides, what we commit to paper we are more likely to remember.

Leafing through my little sketchbooks of the past three decades, I can remember every one of the drawings in them. The flight I was on, the country I was in, who I was with, the mood. It's still there, and still influencing me even today, like a cheat sheet that was not needed after all.

Perhaps there's even a fourth level, which would be that of illustration or cartoons. After all, I often exaggerate things, take a subject and make ten illustrations out of it. The first time I did that was for a Camper boutique in Paris, where I filled the walls with cartoons on the theme of shoes, Camper itself, and Mallorca as the place where it is headquartered. That led to a contract from a car magazine lasting several years and to a regular column in the *Z* magazine of the *NZZ* that I wrote for a year.

Italo Lupi

Question No. 15

worked in graphic design and
architecture in Milan
and was editor–in–chief of the monthly
magazine *Abitare* for sixteen years.

I liked Bruno Munari's works, so how could I not love yours?

My question is as follows: To what extent was your work influenced by artists like Bruno and the novelty of freedom with which Italian design unshackled

Alfredo Häberli

itself from an international style that had degenerated into routine? The idiom of Achille and Piergiacomo Castiglioni must have been music to your ears and undoubtedly a source of inspiration. Is that so?

What I learned from Bruno Munari, Achille Castiglioni, and many others was lightness of touch: how to make air visible, how to be witty and mischievous, how to listen to stories, and how to tell them. Some other things those wonderful people and designers taught me were modesty, dignity, and humility. While I must have had what it takes, they were my idols and they were the ones who set the bar for how I would like to be at their age, with a few decades of work behind me.

I once ran into Achille Castiglioni while waiting for a streetcar in Milan. I was standing right next to him without even realizing it and was too shy to say anything. But I knew him from his products and I knew his face from the portrait stamped on his products for Zanotta. Another random encounter was in 1985 in the foyer of the Museum für Gestaltung in Zurich, where he was showing his world-famous exhibition from Vienna. Ten years later it was the turn of Bruno Munari's exhibition, and ten years after that my own. My engagement with Bruno went very deep, as I was the one who curated that major exhibition of his and edited the tie-in publication.

To help finance my studies I had designed exhibitions for the Museum für Gestaltung even as a student, and eventually they invited me to work on the content of the exhibitions too. My proposal of an exhibition devoted to the work of Bruno Munari and Enzo Mari was accepted and I spent two years working on the content. At first I worked on them both, until it became clear that two such independent–minded personalities really warranted exhibitions of their own. After that I concentrated on Munari, who at first remained aloof, unengaged, as if biding his time. But I did not have to wait long before he let me peek inside every one of his drawers and hanging files, where I discovered things that had never been published.

Bruno also taught me Italian, if only because I read so many of his books, and he has this gift for writing very simply. His observations and little inventions were as simple as they were amazing. And they made such perfect sense that you were constantly asking yourself: How come no one thought of that before? Achille Castiglioni also possessed this gift: the gift of questioning things, viewing the familiar in a new light, seeing the same thing with new eyes. Or to quote Umberto Eco's blurb for *Far vedere l'Aria:* "Munari the man has to have a thousand eyes, on nose and neck, on his shoulders, his fingers, and his behind. A troubled spirit, he rebelled against a world that was bombarding him with stimuli from all directions. By working through the programmatic wisdom of the exact sciences, he discovered himself as a restless inhabitant of an expanding universe."

But it was this world, a world which I, too, discovered in Milan, and which helped allay my yearning for my native Argentina, that opened up the new and enriching world of design for me. It was my safety valve in light of "form follows function," and my training at the Hochschule für Gestaltung, which was no less valuable, but never had the lightness of touch of a Munari or the Castiglioni brothers. Such a paean to freedom and pleasure I could wholeheartedly embrace, it being part of my DNA as an Argentinian. It really is the only way to live: with humor and with humanity.

Another thing I learned from Bruno is how to find a thousand forms of inspiration in nature, in an object, in a line, in an image; and how to act on that inspiration. From Achille Castiglioni I learned to identify the intelligence of objects and to transfer it to other objects. And from both I learned to love life and to love what I do every day, which is to have and find ideas.

I did not do the exhibition about Enzo Mari, even though we were friends. Enzo with his critical and cultural stance taught me very different things, though to write about all that I would need a different question.

Anna Moldenhauer

Question No. 16

is a journalist and heads
the editorial department of
Stylepark magazine
in Frankfurt am Main.

Alfredo, why is intuitive drawing such a crucial form of expression for you in the creation of your designs?

I have a visual memory. At home I have some 35 meters of bookshelves and I know every single page of every single book on them. When I get started on a project, I generally have dozens of pictures swirling around in my head, so the first thing I do is to begin sketching, even drawing things that at first seem to make no sense at all. Just how important those sketches were to the end product often becomes apparent only when I'm finished.

Alfredo Häberli

The hand holding the pencil connects mind and body. Drawing helps me to switch off the mind and the moment I start thinking my drawing falters, because the flow has been interrupted. So I try not to think when drawing. That makes it demanding, but also very interesting. You have to learn to trust both hand and pencil. If I let the line flow without thinking about it, I can actually feel an idea coming on in the pencil. There I am, drawing away, and suddenly an idea manifests itself! I don't judge it for as long as I'm drawing it, but I certainly feel it coming!

Often I can imagine what the pencil is about to draw and can see where the line is leading about five centimeters ahead. But there are also times when even I am totally surprised at what a sketch brings to light. That's why I'm against drawing on the computer too early on in the design process. Because if you draw on the computer, you have to know in advance what you're going to draw. A pencil, by contrast, allows for uncertainty. And ultimately, the energy of freehand drawing will be apparent in the finished product. It will not look "contrived."

A sketch is a highly condensed matter. The art of sketching consists in achieving maximum expressiveness with as few lines as possible. If it helps you get to the heart of the matter, a sketch has succeeded. It's important not to cramp up when sketching. The pencil must sit loosely in the hand. Paul Klee once wrote that sketching is like going for a walk with a pencil. Which is a perfect description of what I do every day: I go for a walk with a pencil! This discovery was the inspiration for the name of the wing–back chair that I created for Moroso in Italy: Take a Line for a Walk.

Question No. 17

Francesca Molteni

is a philosopher, author of films, and founded the Muse Factory of Projects in Milan.

These days we talk a lot about inclusion. Why is it still so difficult for women to rise to the top in architecture and design?

That's a question that pertains not just to architecture and design, a question that has been with us since the 1920s and 1930s and is still an issue today. As a boy I was surrounded by some really great women, whose character, biography, and approach to life were to be a lasting influence on me. Among them were my grandmother and my mother, my father's aunt, and my best friends' mothers. Later, during my time at vocational school and my apprenticeship as an architectural draftsman, my written assignments on theoretical subjects introduced me to artists like Meret Oppenheim, Sophie Taeuber–Arp ("I don't always want to be at the stove"), Emma Kunz, and Switzerland's best–known living woman artist, Pipilotti Rist. I had just turned twenty when I went to an exhibition opening and spent the whole evening with Meret Oppenheim. I didn't actually know who she was, but her amiable and very direct manner, her opinions, and her charisma made a huge impression on me. A short time later I bought a copy of the Italian magazine *Domus* No. 605 with Oppenheim on the cover and felt myself being beamed up into a world that seemed as surreal as her works, certainly not of the here and now.

There were very few women in architecture and design when I was a student. Only when I began working in Scandinavia a good twenty years ago did I find myself in a world in which women's involvement in design was taken for granted. And that had been achieved deliberately, but naturally, not with quotas. And they were in the majority!

At Iittala, Kvadrat, and Georg Jensen I dealt almost exclusively with women—and at all levels and in the most diverse fields, always as a matter of course.

answers a question by Francesca Molteni

The highlight for me was a dinner that I organized called "9 + 1 is more than 10." The men were let in only for the after–dinner drinks, though since I was the host, I was allowed to stay. The women were very different and didn't know each other beforehand, so it was exciting to see them interact. Sadly that was to be the only edition of that legendary dinner party—and of course I would have loved to have my wife Stefanie there, too. Then the new formula would have been "10 + 1 = 9 + 2H."

Why women are still underrepresented in architecture and design also has to do with the possibilities and structures offered to mothers and fathers by the state and society in general, and the assumptions made of them. The Nordic countries are exemplary here and practice a model that allows women, or rather mothers, to get back to work very quickly. But the patriarchy in many countries is still so dominant that it will take years for any kind of equality to be reached.

As I already said, I had the good fortune to work with some impressive women, with Patrizia Moroso, Sandra Severi Sarfatti, Adelaide Acerbi Astori, Louise Langkilde, Anne Højgaard Jørgensen, Njusja de Gier, Stine

Find Osthe, and many others in our sector of the design industry. It's a different way of working in that the primary concern is always the task in hand, not status or your position in the hierarchy. The content is what counts. That is something I learned from them and have practiced vis–à–vis my clients in my studio ever since day one: "Say what you do. Do what you say. And be what you do"—even if that calls for courage, and accordingly for humility. That is what I've always done, and still do today, with my mother, my wife, and with all the women I know. And with men, too, even if they sometimes struggle with it, being still stuck in competitive mode.

I love looking at the works of Charlotte Perriand, Eileen Grey, Sophie Taeuber–Arp, Louise Bourgeois, Lina Bo Bardi, Gae Aulenti, Barbara Hepworth, Katharina Grosse, Rosemarie Trockel, and Agnes Martin, and take great pleasure in their oeuvres. But when I read their CVs, I sometimes feel sick at heart and am ashamed of the way we men treated them.

Question No. 18

Hans Ulrich Obrist

is artistic director of the Serpentine Galleries in London and previously of the Musée d'Art Moderne de la Ville de Paris.

What are your unrealized projects?

Right now I'm working on a partially unrealized project, which is the thirtieth anniversary of my studio. Over the past three decades I've had the good fortune to meet some wonderful people, including many artists, architects, designers, and producers. These encounters have remained with me, shaping my life, and influencing what I do in my studio. During the Covid–19 pandemic, this wonderful phase of discovery, of meeting new people, was reduced to zero. For the first time since 1986 I was not at the furniture fair in Milan. And this hiatus seems to me to reflect what the furniture industry itself is going through, namely a pause, a period of reflection, a transformation, a moment of relief from the stranglehold of ever more, ever faster, ever more international. This time–out has forced us to do some hard thinking. I myself would like to write about it—though not about me personally, my life, my biography, even if this phase of my life is bound to be part of it. What really interest me are the wonderful people I have gotten to know, people who are sadly entering that phase in which they must bid farewell to life with all the sorrow that that entails. So that is one unrealized project that I am currently working on.

The situation within the furniture design business has also been on my mind. How come marketing is the real winner of the past few decades? Why aren't we designers critical enough? And why do journalists no longer write about these things? We like to call ourselves an "innovative industry," but what do we actually do, apart from study annual sales figures? Isn't there an excess of opportunism? Could it be shrunk to arrive at a stable state? Would that even be possible?

So to stay with your question: Another unrealized project might be a collection born of a visibly different stance, one that still has rough edges, that perhaps is not commercial, that is manifesto-like. I'm not talking about a new Memphis syndrome, though it's certainly high time. So how do I shake people up? How do I talk about such things? And how can I prevent the outcome from becoming all too formal? A three–dimensional manifesto, that's what I have in mind; that's what transports me into the realm of unrealized projects. It would be nice to work on such a project together with my friends—friends from many different fields, who nevertheless share the same spirit, for whom the content is what counts. As long as it's divorced from its own context, it will work, but as soon as extraneous circumstances intervene— the terms of contract, industry, hierarchies— then it will no longer work.

Freer projects are also interesting, aren't they? And yet context, and the constraints of context, has always fascinated me, and challenged me. Otherwise I would have become an artist.

For some years now I have been working with a team on a golf set. The project is an inquiry into how the game might be simplified and the set pared down to its essentials, although its joint–relieving properties have already resulted in a patent. So we're again talking about achieving something within the constraints of context. These are projects that take years to see through to completion. The golf set, for example, has been ticking over since the first contact in 2016.

There are other unrealized projects, too: a children's book, a sailboat, and a watch—though with any luck the latter should be finished by the time this book goes to print.

Question No. 19

Francesca Picchi

is an architect and
journalist living
in Milan, and teaches design
history in Florence.

Given the increasingly homogeneous panoply of goods and products on offer, is there something akin to biodiversity* that could be applied to industrial products?

Fortunately, the changes of perception in design that I myself have witnessed make it easier for me to answer this highly complex question. The fact is that the globalization of the design business

*By biodiversity I mean the differentiation of individuals of the same species in relation to environmental factors.

and its pursuit of growth have gone hand in hand with a homogenization of aesthetics. This is in part a consequence of the same designers working for different companies, though it also has to do with the trendsetting role played by the same lead manufacturers. In other words, we have seen aesthetics and quality gradually align, while marketing has gained the upper hand.

This process of alignment, however, underestimates just how different our customs, traditions, and histories are. The significance of a dining table, say, is different in Spain than in Scandinavia, since the family structures (patriarchy), meanings, materials, and climatic conditions in these two places are themselves very different. Fortunately, thanks to digitalization, the past fifteen years have seen personalization—that is, customization—become much more readily accessible.

In this current phase of reduce, recycle, and reuse, a phase focused on sustainability and environmental challenges, we have had to accustom ourselves to a new reality. If we are to create things that are genuinely new, overhaul our supply chains, and transform our economic structures, we first have to develop new business models and new technologies. Viewed in this light, I find myself transported back to the 1980s (Memphis, Postmodernism, The New Spirit). What counts today is once again imagination, an enterprising spirit, and above all hard work.

Biodiversity is defined by the larger context. The design industry will have to adapt if it is to survive, and what we are in the midst of now is this same dynamic phase of adaptation.

Valentina Raggi

Question No. 20

is a journalist with a passionate curiosity for design and its crossings with the wider panorama of the contemporary disciplines. She lives in Milan, writes for a number of different magazines, and is senior editor at *AD Italia*.

Your world is a playful and self-conscious cosmos. Multidisciplinarity, ecology, quantum leaps, and irony are necessary concepts these days, but you have always had them in your DNA. What will be the new symbolic object of tomorrow?

Alfredo Häberli

Whenever I get lucky, I appreciate it and am grateful for it. This fundamentally positive outlook is a character trait that many Argentinians share. It is a virtue that to me seems necessary to survival. Politics is so awful and so dishonest, and business so wretched and so dubious, that taking each day as it comes and living in the moment knowing that what comes next is anything but certain hones your sense of humor and is a great survival strategy—humor and wit, joy and passion.

What you say about my work sounds right to me. I see the elegance of curiosity and irony in my products, and that they can be meaningful without being loud and shrill. But I also have a very critical streak in me and this has helped me not to become conceited or to see myself as a star designer. So I'm glad of that side of myself, too.

And you are also right to say that designers should also enjoy what they do. Because design can be fun! It should be fun, even if it also calls for self–awareness, responsibility, critique, not so much self–adulation, but definitely enjoyment! We should also take our work seriously, especially in these uncertain times of ours when our own habitat is in peril. I've consistently heeded my heart, my passion, and my intuition over the past twenty years, and this, I believe, is the only way to address the problems now facing us, solving which will require tremendous strength and willpower.

What I'm trying to say is this: It is the things that bother us, that touch us, that get us all worked up, the things that get under our skin and that keep us awake at night that we should be tackling. It's only when we commit to things like that that we derive true pleasure from our work, as do artists who cannot help themselves, or researchers, or athletes. But can I learn such a lightness of touch? Can I school myself to enjoy conceptual work? I try to convey happiness both in my objects and in my own person. But is it enough? Does it carry any weight at all? I don't know.

So if I were to choose just one symbolic object, it would be a mirror, and if I were to stand in front of it, I would ask myself: Is the mirror being honest with me? Because that honest answer would be the answer I was looking for and on which I would then act.

Question No. 21

Alice Rawsthorn

writes about design in London.

What is design? And what should it be?

Everything and nothing. It is a concept that is not even that old but has already been diluted. Design is sometimes actually a pejorative. But for me it is first and foremost the profession that I found for myself, that I can live from, and that for me comes to life anew every single day, keeping me busy and making me happy. As a designer I see things, contemplate the world, and grapple with themes that I could never have dreamed of. Design enables me to see the world.

Yet I am not obsessive. I take it as it comes.

I respect pluralism in design and would never claim that there is only ever one valid solution. We humans are simply too different for that. Hence my suspicion of any form of doctrine or indeed any narrowing or rigidity, even if I need them to define my own stance, my own ethic. Just as I always admit the other, the other way of seeing, since there is never only one truth, though I stand for mine.

Design is the search for ideas that lead to a form and that ideally should touch us, eliciting an emotion, prompting reflection. Design is not about design. Design is about life, which is what its content should be too.

Question No. 22

Sandra Reichl

is a brand strategist and designer who lives and works in Vienna and founded the creative consultancy Apt.

What is passion and what is success?

If I were to define passion in words, it would be as follows: Say what you feel, and do what you think, day in, day out.

Success is when what we imagine, dream, and desire actually happens, whatever it happens to be.

For me, success has never been a monetary matter.

Erik Rimmer

Question No. 23

is editor–in–chief
of several Scandinavian magazines,
such as *Bo Bedre*
from Denmark and Norway.

I think of you more than once a week. In fact, I salute you every time I drink wine out of a glass from your Essence collection for littala. What was your starting point for that design process?

And is there anything you would do differently today?

I was so desperate to create something new that I really suffered during that design process. Of course that's always my ambition, but in that particular instance I somehow lost myself in my search for a modern, contemporary form. The end result, Essence, has three salient characteristics: a flat foot, a slightly conical and extra thin stem measuring just five millimeters in diameter at the transition to the cup, and then the various cups with their rhomboid, masculine–looking forms. The key question was this: Which and how many glasses do I need at home?

My first presentation of the design was very amusing, as I was asked whether this was my first glass design. Being both clueless and proud I answered in the affirmative—and everyone rolled their eyes! I was told that such a design was simply impossible to make, which was quite a blow. But the technicians and engineers took up the challenge and developed a new quality of glass specially for my design. And there it was: an invisible invention.

Nearly two years later, in 2001, I was asked to approve the glass forms before they went into production. Three days had been set aside for this purpose, so off I flew to Finland. For the first glass presented to me, the largest of the series, I wanted to raise the foot to five millimeters. There were murmurs of complaint. The young designer was at it again—coming up with impossible ideas!

We then had a breakout session with the team of technicians and they agreed to my wish. The consequence of this, however, was that twenty different tools had to be changed overnight! I didn't sleep at all that night, but to my great surprise, everyone was in a good mood next day. It turned out that the change I had demanded had solved many other problems that they had been having. The other glasses were fine and I was able to wave them through.

Essence became the most inspiring glass of the last twenty years and an icon of design. Twenty-five thousand of them are produced in a single day.

To mark the twentieth anniversary we supplemented the collection with a set made of pressed glass and porcelain. According to Kaj

Franck's *Thema*, Essence is one of Iittala's two best-selling collections. So no, I wouldn't do anything differently!

Marco Sammicheli

Question No. 24

is a curator at the
Triennale and director of the Museo del Design
Italiano in Milan, and likes
sacred architecture and good food.

How would you describe the unknown?

The unknown, the intuitive spirit, is a sacred gift, and a true servant of our powers of reasoning. I think we live in a society that honors the servant but forgets the gift. Gerd Gigerenz said something along those lines, and I can only concur.

The unknown is something in between intuition and spiritual intelligence. It is a feeling, something that cannot be expressed in words—in pictures, if anything; visually or musically. But even just the desire to describe the unknown destroys that same vacuum, that state of not knowing, that incognito that is so pronounced in little children. It's a feeling we might get under the bed or under the table, as a child all on its own. But it can also give rise to a work of art, and be felt when that work is contemplated.

Alfredo Häberli

The unknown probably cannot be grasped. Otherwise it would not be unknown. It is empty, weightless, exotic, nameless; a color somewhere between white and transparent; air. You've asked me a very beautiful, very poetic and philosophical question. Is it mystical? Can it be the future?

Unendingly unknown? It looks like this one is going to remain unanswered.

Gunda Siebke

Question No. 25

holds a degree in design
and heads the design department
of *Schöner Wohnen*
magazine in Hamburg.

What have you done wrong?

Thirty years ago, I founded my own design studio, and last year, during the pandemic, I did a lot of thinking. It was a watershed moment—so much changed within a single month. The world held its breath. Everybody was hit by it.

I began to write a book about the many different people I've been lucky enough to meet and my encounters with them. That led me to ask myself what I've been doing with my life, and all at once I felt insecure—am I too radical? I work only with people I like. And I've coined my own motto, which is: "Say what you do. Do what you say. And be what you do." I'd dreamed of working for certain firms right from the start, from 1986 when I first attended the furniture fair in Milan. Yes, it helps to be persistent in your wishes,

because I've since been able to work for eight of
the original ten I set my sights on.

But some of these same firms are no longer in the hands of the families that founded them. In fact, they were in family hands for just one generation, if that. Too many family members wanted to have a stake in them and feed off them. These days almost all of them belong to investment groups—anonymous players that prioritize profits and have no appreciation of design as a cultural asset. Not that making money doesn't matter; all good industrialists have that in their DNA, and without that blend of courage and humility they would not have been successful. Their priority was innovation, our cultural heritage.

So many things have fallen apart and last year, with time on my hands and no business trips scheduled, I had an opportunity to think about this. I wondered if I should stop going out on a limb? Be ready to make more compromises? Be more calculating, more strategic—more dishonest even? That was what was going through my head; and I thought maybe I'd got it all wrong, though I couldn't have taken a different path in any case, despite that sudden moment of insecurity. No, no way, I had followed my intuition and with it run the risk of losing everything, which is another of the industrialist's virtues!

So have I done anything wrong?
What can anyone do wrong?

Question No. 26

David Streiff Corti

is now a freelance writer and teacher in Zurich and wrote for many years for the *Neue Zürcher Zeitung* on the subject of design.

When did you first realize that you might just make it?

If I had to single out just one event, it would be my graduation project at the Hochschule für Gestaltung in 1991, which won me the Hochschule Prize for the best graduation project submitted that year. For someone who had been admitted to the program only at the second attempt that was a real vindication. Not only was I in seventh heaven, but the prize also laid the foundation stone of my design studio, which I opened two days later.

It also convinced me that if I approached my contracts just like I had that graduation project, I would be able to do great things. That passion, that dedication, that refusal to compromise guaranteed a standard far above the average. Receiving that boost encouraged me to work for foreign clients too. The prospect of one day working for Italian furniture–makers had enthralled me ever since 1986, and a few years later I was doing just that. Successes both large and small followed and presumably played a role in building up my confidence. But the defeats were even more instructive and I grew with each new setback.

Question No. 27

Robert Thiemann

is founder
and director of Frame,
a global platform
for interior design in
Amsterdam.

How has your focus changed over the past thirty years?

I hope it has shifted, because for the first ten years I worked day and night, seven days a week. Then came my international breakthrough and all the work that I had put in began to pay off in the form of royalties. It was then, fortunately, that my wife and I decided to have children, meaning that the next ten years were dominated by the challenge of balancing the demands of the studio with those of raising a family. Then came the calmer, but more concentrated, more intense period of the past ten years. The breadth and variety of the work I have done to date is immense. I've managed to stay cool and have enjoyed the complex projects just as much as the smaller, easier ones. This mixture, the different mentalities of the different countries in which I work—it's like a dream come true.

At first I was happy just to be working for industry at all. Every object that went into production was another tiny piece of a much larger puzzle. Every experience brought new knowledge, knowledge that I cannot imagine being without. Sometimes it's debilitating, but mostly it's of service to the matter in hand. So many things have changed in the various sectors in which I work: in furniture, architecture, the automotive industry. The greatest changes have undoubtedly been in communications and digitalization, and even more crucially in the environment—not to forget the pandemic.

I am very privileged and have doubtless achieved a great deal. I can work on the things that interest me—though I've been doing that all along—and through my know-how and the name I've made for myself, I'm now much better placed to have a say on the matter in hand. My industrial clients, I notice, are invariably surprised to discover that what matters to me is not my ego, but the content, a particular stance, transparency and integrity. Being famous as a designer is really not so important to me. So this focus is perhaps what has changed most since I first opened my studio.

Paolo Tumminelli

Question No. 28

studied architecture, rushed through marketing, and ended up stranded as a design professor in Cologne.

Imagine your previous life was just a dream and you wake up in a world in which the automobile has not yet been invented. You have to imagine it from scratch. What do you see?

The object, the machine, would be created with wonderful human intelligence and would make respectful use of nature to drive it along, harnessing wind like a sailing ship or a kite–powered vehicle. It would glide over vast expanses—an ocean or a desert—and would be elegant, fluid, with large, silky smooth curves. It would be designed from the inside out and would make its occupant feel safe, as if gliding along in a cocoon or on a sofa. It would be largely transparent but at the same time allow for privacy. In appearance it would look like a cross between a sailing ship, an aircraft, and a car. But it still lacks definition, and since it doesn't yet exist cannot be described exactly. Think of something between a shark, a dolphin, and a seagull.

What fascinates me is not the artificial intelligence, but rather the mechanical experience. I see a group of people in it—a family, say—rather than a single person. I see its outer shell as white or silver and slightly reflective. It reflects both its surroundings and the sky, which makes it slightly less transparent.

A few years ago I was able to work on just such a question for real, and I called my vehicle and the concept that I came up with The Sphere—Perspectives in Precision & Poetry. The precision is human intelligence coupled with the non–linearity of nature and poetry.

Ramón Úbeda

Question No. 29

is art director and consultant at
several Spanish companies,
including Andreu World, Camper, and
BD Barcelona.

How important is it to have fun when creating— from the first idea to the naming of your work?

The German word for fun, *Spass,* is used a lot, sometimes too much. What I can certainly say is that the profession I chose for myself is one that I find lots of fun. I wake up every day looking forward to the challenges facing me at the studio, even if sometimes they're not much fun at all, though that, too, is part of the process. My childhood in Argentina and my parents had a formative influence on me. South America's political and economic woes are bearable only with a sense of humor, a positive mindset, and persistence. You just have to hope for a brighter future. So having fun is definitely relevant, essential even—and not just fun but joy!

I've had to work on myself and learn to cope quickly with setbacks ever since my teenage years. Because to have ideas I have to be doing well, have to be in the flow. Of course the obstacles, the problems, the challenges of any given process are just as exciting, and overcoming them, solving them, can also be fun. At the studio I always tell my assistants that we should set the bar high that we intend to leap over. The history of what is there also has a bearing on this. But then, to stay with the same metaphor, every step we take toward the bar, the pace we run at, and the contortions we perform there (sometimes backward!) are essential to our being able to leap over it. And doing that over and over again can be fun— every time!

Of course, the routine work involved in creativity isn't always fun. It's often a hard-won pleasure. But enjoying what you do is fundamental to being able to do it well.

If you giggle or chuckle or snigger at least seventeen times a day, you'll laugh five hundred

thousand times in the course of your life—
or so I read in a newspaper just recently.

And that, too, made me laugh!

Question No. 30

Marco Velardi

founded the consultancy Apartemento in Berlin and speaks the language of attentive people.

If you had to describe your own personality in terms of food, how would that description read and why?

A portrait of myself like those painted by Renaissance artist Giuseppe Arcimboldo? A surreal composition of fruits, vegetables, flowers, and fish? My godchild used to make fun of my stature and called me "the beanpole." As a native of Argentina, beef inevitably springs to mind, because beef was omnipresent throughout my childhood, and I, too, am made of meat. But my personality? Described in terms of food?

Over the years I've acquired a kind of protective shell as a defense against becoming all things to all people, because people do have this tendency to take what they want without heeding your privacy. So you could say that I have a thin outer skin, like an apple or a banana; or perhaps an even finer and softer one, like a peach, steeped in warm sunshine and sweetness, intense in color, but with a hard kernel. As a man I am all those things; and undoubtedly a humanist, since humanism is a philosophy that turns on human well-being and that champions human freedom, autonomy, and progress. I'm definitely a people person and I have a big heart. I would say that I'm an amiable fellow, with a lot of respect for others, as also for the world of nature, and for the environment. I can also be harsh, though only when it's a matter of fairness or content—or my personal vision or image. And even then, only if it makes sense, not for the sake of it or simply to satisfy my own ego. I often withdraw, too.

So perhaps I would be a salad, with peaches, tomatoes, and mozzarella, garnished with peppermint—if it has to be a whole dish, that is.

But the idea of myself as a peach—
that fits.

Acknowledgments

The concept for this book entailed switching roles so that for once I would be the one answering the questions. Thirty people from architecture and design asked me one question each, and answering them turned out to be a very interesting experience. The reactions varied greatly from the joyful and witty to the hesitant and pleading, from the intelligent and even arrogant to the baldly polite. Some questions were incredibly difficult and philosophical. A certain amount of repetition was unavoidable, but I'm deeply grateful for the wide–ranging themes that my interlocutors touched on—and for their arrival in time for my studio's thirtieth anniversary.

Imprint

Concept **Alfredo Häberli**
Editing of the German texts **Ursula Eichenberger**
Translations **Bronwen Saunders**
Design **DelerueRoppel**
Printing and binding **Offizin Scheufele**

© 2024 Alfredo Häberli and
Verlag Scheidegger & Spiess AG, Zürich

Verlag Scheidegger & Spiess
Niederdorfstrasse 54
8001 Zürich, Switzerland
www.scheidegger-spiess.ch

Scheidegger & Spiess is being supported by
the Federal Office of Culture with a general subsidy
for the years 2021–2024.

All rights reserved; no part of this publication may be reproduced,
stored in a retrieval system or transmitted in any form or
by any means, electronic, mechanical, photocopying, recording,
or otherwise, without the prior written consent of the publisher.

This book is part of the two-volume publication

**Alfredo Häberli—
Verbal Doodling. / 30 Years, Questions, Answers.**

and is not available separately.

ISBN 978-3-03942-115-2

German Edition:

ISBN 978-3-03942-114-5